The Impeded Stream

This book is the second collection of poems from a former Naval Officer and Navy SEAL. Drawing from his extensive world travels, operations, and from the spice of his Southern upbringing and heritage, his work speaks to the vibrancy of life across a myriad of landscapes, lives, and experiences.

Michael R. Howard

The Impeded Stream
Copyright © 2024 Michael R. Howard
First Edition
Printed in the United States
ISBN: 978-1-970153-44-6

No part of this publication may be reproduced or transmitted in any form or by any means, graphic, electronic, photocopy, recording, or by any information storage retrieval system—except for excerpts used for published review—without the written permission of the author.

Distributed by Ingram Book Company

La Maison Publishing
Vero Beach, Florida
The Hibiscus City
lamaisonpublishing@gmail.com

"Michael's thought-provoking poems take us on a multisensory journey to places both exotic and familiar, deep and touching, light and lively. Never too far away from his Southern roots, Michael splashes his poems with visual, auditory, and tactile images that bring a vibrant interpretive warmth to his subjects and themes."

> Susan Lovelace, Editor. Career Educator. The Laura (Riding) Jackson Foundation's Education Coordinator.

"The impeded stream is the one that sings."
Wendell Berry

For
William Patrick and Katherine Marie

Acknowledgments

Grateful acknowledgment is given to the publications and events where the following poems first appeared:

The Lightning and the Gale – 2022 – "Where the Moss Don't Grow"

Ekphrastic Poems:

"Flower of Calvary" Inspired by a stained-glass piece by artist Anita Prentice.

"A Heavenly Scape" inspired by the painting "Provence" by artist Laura Reed Howell.

"Bison on the Wall" inspired by a painting from the collection of artist Eldon Lux.

"Something of Value" inspired by a photograph from the collection of photographer Jennifer Johnson, taken while on safari in Africa.

"Winter Beach" inspired by an article written by Louise Kennedy, after visiting the Winter Beach Cemetery where Laura (Riding) Jackson and her husband are buried.

"Strength of Odysseus" inspired by a sculpture from the collection of Indian River County Poet Laureate Sean Sexton.

A special thanks to these artists for allowing me to use their art in this book.

"Nora, A Student's Lament" awarded Second Place in the 2023 Phenomenal Women Poetry Contest sponsored by the American Association of University Women and the Laura (Riding) Jackson Foundation. I read this at the Emerson Theater on March 19, 2023. It will appear in the forthcoming LRJF Press Chapbook, (an imprint of The Seizin Press), titled *"Phenomenal Women: An Anthology."*

"Death of a War Correspondent" selected for publication in the forthcoming LRJF Press, Chapbook, (an imprint of The Seizin Press), titled *"Phenomenal Women: An Anthology."*

It is again a great pleasure to thank my Editor, Susan Lovelace, and Publisher, Janet Sierzant, for their continued help and support. They continue to make my work far better. I also owe a special thanks to Mr. Richard Morgan, Dr. Jacque Jacobs, and again, Susan Lovelace, for their time and effort to read my draft manuscript and still have the courage to offer such kind remarks about this book and allow me to print their endorsements. Thank you.

Introduction

This book's cover art is a favorite oil painting of mine by Elizabeth Thompson, also known as Lady Butler. She painted this in 1881 and it depicts the start of the cavalry charge of the Royal Scots Greys at the battle of Waterloo in 1815. A copy of this painting has been in my home for decades. Lady Butler stated that she painted this, "Not to glorify war but to show its pathos and heroism." It certainly does this for me as it explodes with energy, bravery, and historical victory. I would like to believe that in another life I was a cavalry officer, overcome by the perceived glory, equine sentiment, and martial beauty of warriors on horseback.

The title of this book is a line from the poem "Our Real Work" by Wendell Berry. It is a simple phrase but profound and very personal. I had other ideas for a title but once I discovered this quote, the title decision was easy.

There are six ekphrastic poems included in this collection. An ekphrastic poem is a vivid description of a scene or a work of art. It can be quite a challenge to produce a poem inspired by a work of art of any kind. However, it is a great creative exercise. I wrote all six of these ekphrastic poems during collaborative events involving local artists and our Laura (Riding) Jackson

Foundation writing groups. I have identified these artists on the "Acknowledgments" page of this book. These collaborative events included a variety of art, such as photography, abstract paintings, watercolor scenes, and stained glass. One I wrote from a person's description of her visit to a local cemetery.

As I did in my first anthology, I included a "Notes" section at the end, which provides context for the poems. I view the use of notes as not unlike visiting an art museum where a docent guides you around and provides a deeper perspective for each piece of art that we might not know or see otherwise. The "Notes" are there to use or not.

The Impeded Stream

Michael R. Howard

Table of Contents

Where the Moss Don't Grow 1

Nora, a Student's Lament 3

I Dream Again of You 5

Night-Blooming Jasmine 7

Ode to Cleavage 9

Flower of Calvary 10

She Carried the Scent of Coffee 12

Rose Dew 13

The Crystal Wind Chime 15

My Virgin Chart 17

A Pirate's Just Deserts 19

A Heavenly Scape 22

Black Beauty 24

Finding Lynyrd Skynyrd 26

They Commanded the Mile 28

Ghost Car 30

Foothill Coyote 32

Bison on the Wall 34

Death of a War Correspondent 37

Wyoming Hunt 40

An Oasis	43
El Paisano	46
Sweet Horchata	48
Something of Value	50
What I Learned from Chip	52
Late Confession	54
Eva Braun's Home Movies	56
My Shot 'a Whiskey	58
Honeymoon Pull-Off	59
Winter Beach	61
The Banshee	63
Petrol in a Puddle	64
What's Uncle Worth	65
Apple Tree Dreams	68
Grandma Squaw	69
Strength of Odysseus	72
The Fall	74
The Forgiving River	75
Sail On	77
My Suzanne	78
Dropping Anchor	80
About the Author	81
Notes	83

Where the Moss Don't Grow

Oh, I cain't live where the moss don't grow.
It'd be too cold and sometime it might snow.
The cypress and oak gotta look old and grey,
And in the wind, gotta whisper and sway.

Some Yankee say he don't like the moss.
Say it block the sun, say the light be lost.
But I cain't live where the moss don't grow.
I like it hangin' round where the black water flow.

Sometime I walk barefoot down that cool sand road,
Through the tunnel of oak, carryin' my load.
That moss be swayin' and I be thinkin' 'bout my girl,
And that moss be flowin' like her long dark curl.

Now in the spring when the 'zalia
Blaze round the trunk,
I pick that pink blossom and with a kiss jus' fo' luck,
Place it in that grey-flowin' moss and curl,
And know I'm rich beyond diamond and pearl.

Now my sista say that moss be the beards
Of all them dead rebels them Yankees feared.
Say they gotta hang forever for all to see
That them rebel spirits still roam free.

But my Mama say that ain't right,
Say the moon weave that moss on a cold, dark night,
When the wind blow hard from out the north,
And the river rise up, and the fear come forth.

Say the moon weave that moss
For a lost Seminole child,
Whose mother climbed the high cypress
And cried aloud
To a hidden moon for mercy
On her child so young.
So the moon weave that moss
While that hurricane sung.

Now that child was spared, kept safe thru the night,
While in that moss wrapped warm and tight.
Then the moon come out, see the work of his hand,
And so pleased, spread that moss
Cross his favored land.

So, I won't live where that moss don't grow.
I like it hangin' round me in this ole boat I row.
I like the way it dress up the pine.
I like that moss, I like it jus' fine.

Nora, a Student's Lament

You were rare indeed, Nora,
A Miss, I hoped, when you clicked in
On high heels with unusual confidence and class,
Sat on your desk, not behind it.
A short skirt, unique for our teachers,
Showcased muscular legs and strong thighs,
Peeked and tweaked my adolescent interest.
Your auburn hair pulled tight,
With a youthful tie in back
While an air of erotic sophistication engulfed
Our class like heavy smoke from a smoldering fire.
Your indifference amped my romantic daydreams.

You pushed your glasses up and back,
Stylish and brazen.
Then you spoke.

Not syrup southern we had dulled into daily,
Nor prudish and provincial like the others,
But European: German, Austrian perhaps.
A mysterious goddess here to shove
Latin, German, and mythology
Down our lowly throats.

Then, your ancient gods spoke to me.
I befriended Homer, set sail in the Iliad and Odyssey.
Apollo sang to us. I slept with Edith Hamilton.
Nora, you were my Venus. As Neptune,

I lured you to my lair by the sea.

You opened Europe to us, and the war.
Told us of your lover, a young soldier,
Lost somewhere in the fight and chaos.
He had a special tattoo on his shoulder.
You searched for him. Had he forgotten you?
Then at Leipzig med school you saw
The cadaver with that special tattoo.

Years later I searched for you.
I wanted to show you what I had become,
The places I had been, things I had seen.
You'd had hope for me, saw promise,
Admired my restless spirit, my interests.
You had inspired me.
I needed to tell you.

But our Gods left long ago.
Only Apollo sang quietly in the distance.
You had grown old, lost somewhere, too.
If only you'd had a special tattoo.

Ah, but Nora,
I am still Neptune.
And you are still with me
In my lair by the sea.

I Dream Again of You

Where are you now?
Who are you?
You, who sweetly haunt my dreams,
A pleasant haunt indeed.
Eagerly I seek the sleep that
Brings you again to me
Where I see you clearly
Through the night haze.
I know you then, want you,
Clutch at your perfections.

Do I haunt your nights, too?
Are you out there,
Asleep, too, in search of me
In your night dreams?
Do we meet and our
Minds and souls collide?
Will we one day
Embrace, entwine?
Are our mortal selves
Equal to our dreams?

Should we meet,
Will we know the other
And in that instant
Know that love of dreams?
Will our lust be real,
Our passion as sweet,

Our desire burn as long?
Should I travel the world
In search of that one
Chance encounter?

Night-Blooming Jasmine

I stood and gazed at the stars
The light winter breeze
Lifted the night jasmine
Sweetly past, filling the street
Where anxious shadows danced,
Cast by the soft, street light
Hidden among the untrimmed
Palms and low branches
Of the old oak.

She stopped, startled: as if
Confronted by a stranger,
An unseen threat. She held her head
High and back, searched the air,
Face into the soft wind.
I knew that look, searching, searching,
Like a hungry wolf on the scent of a mate.
Closer she came
To my shadow.
 "Ahh," she whispered softly.
"I know that fragrance now,
Night-Blooming Jasmine."

She then saw the thickness of the vine,
How it engulfed the pine,
Clutched it, filled it, held it all too tightly.
"Oh, how I love you."

Then, she was gone.
The dark night absorbed her.
The night jasmine bloomed on
A few more days.
Then, too, was gone.

Ode to Cleavage

You invite my attentions
With the natural splendor
Of a glacier's open crevasse.
You tempt and tease
With the same intrigue and danger
That lures one to explore its depth.

My arrogance says you invite.
But that Siren of desire deceives.
It is only the eternal, covetous thoughts,
Deadly as a blue-iced glacial scar
Or hot as Mount Vesuvius.

Gold and silver enhance all,
Subtle, seductive, mysterious.
Perfumed, I am the hungry bee.
If buttressed to impress; it does.

Touch the ancient blue-ice scar,
Plunge in, be slapped
With a lifetime of pain,
Maybe.

Secret glances please, perhaps both.
Jewels draw the eyes like a matador's cape.
But she holds the sword
For the *coup de grace*.

Flower of Calvary

Flamboyant Flame of the Forest,
Phoenix Flower of Haiphong,
Harbinger of the Monsoon,
Mistress of the Marianas,
King of the Keys.
Delonix Regia,
Royal Poinciana.
The Flower of Calvary.

High above lush green, fern-like shade
The Osprey sits and sways
On feathery limbs and leaves
Of pinnae to pinnule,
While seed pods, big as skis,

Hang like Nubian Goat ears,
Their rattle demands release
To march on,
Far from their birth
In Madagascar.

Flame Tree, Forest Peacock,
Envy of sunrise and sunset,
Demander of artists' amour
Who kiss her on canvas
And on stained glass mosaics.
They set her ablaze in eternal June;
She roars her royal colors.

Yet once, humbly she stood
In the shadow of the cross.
No shade nor
Ornamental delight to offer.
But Christ's blood,
Crimson and bright,
Splashed her petals.
Forgiven, transformed, free,
She is…The Flower of Calvary.

She Carried the Scent of Coffee

She carried the scent of coffee
With her through the rest of that day.
Our words had sweetened
The dark, bitter taste that had
Come through the door with her,
Out of the cold, grey day.

She shed her heavy coat
That cloaked and weighed
On her slim shoulders,
And a new warmth
Coursed through her veins,
For a short while.

We talked vaguely of
A sun setting too early,
The days warmth
Cooling too quickly;
Talk that began too late,
Ended too soon.

If only the scent of coffee
Could restore energy to her life;
Heal, not steal her strength;
And make her tears
Fall from laughter,
Not from what is supposed to cure,
Not mistaken for crying.

Rose Dew

She called it Rose Dew,
Where the tide swells into the salt marsh,
Fills the flats like the innocent swelling of our hearts.
We sat in the dock swing as the water lapped the pilings,
Gently, quietly, soothing the silence and expectations.
Channel lights kept time with our quickened pulse
As lights of passing tugs winked knowingly
Through the nodding palm fronds further out.

The heavy wake of a passing barge welled up
To embrace the thick spartina, lift us,
As our thoughts swelled, too, grew inside,
But stopped short in our throats while we searched the stars
For answers that were not there, that never came.
Fingers interlocked, thighs touched and that warmth
Remains forever with her fragrance of that night when
Savannah lights grew ever dimmer with the coming light.

The Vernon River flows on past Moon River,
Merges seamlessly with Little Ogeechee
And together they melt into the sea.
I felt we would be one, too,
And flow easily into the future. But
She could not see my eyes in the darkness

And I had no words,
For they were too far away.

I thought I'd come back often to Rose Dew
But it was sold and the swing I see
Only in a far-off memory.
But I taste the salt air of that night
And her fragrance resumes each time
I walk a creaking dock over the salt marsh
And put my hand in the tepid waters
And feel the warmth of her thigh.

The Crystal Wind Chime

She spoke to me
On a soft summer day
When the sun lingered
And the ferry was late.

We waited, unhurried,
Glad for time to breathe
The salt air and doze
And laugh in the shade
At silly things said and

Absorb the moment
As the winds whispered
Through the pines
And froze a sound
In my mind like a photo
That I recall with the same

Clarity that tickled
The air in the stillness
Of that simple day
When the purest notes
From a crystal wind chime,
Hung from a low branch,
Sweetened the day's weight.

I have searched years
For another simple sound
To speak to me as it did,
But the ferry is never late now.

My Virgin Chart

Unfurl my old virgin chart,
My ageless love,
Of distant paper seas.
Breathe new life
Into her memory.
Reveal her mysterious forms,
Her sweet-scented islands, exotic shores,
Gold-laden wrecks below,
Rusting remnants of battles, of storms.
Unleash her promise.
Feel her smoothness in the red dark and
Warm glow of our wild, bucking bridge.
Softly touch her cool, high latitudes,
Her hot sere of Cancer, Capricorn,
Her wet heat between.
Hold down her eager edges
Against the four winds' fury.
Heed her compass rose,
Her fathomed depths.
Steer clear her rocks, her shoals,
Her reefs and wrecks.
Embrace her currents' curves,
Her surging pulse of tide,
Her rising breath of storm.
Inhale her cleanness,
Fragrance of a new love,
Promise of a new voyage.
Trust her with

A salty pilot's eye,
Dreams of prior sailors' love.
Plot our way ahead,
With stiff Rum,
To where our rhumb line ends.
Take one last round of bearings,
For a three-point fix,
One last view of home, "Aye"
"Bearing, mark, three five six."
Set and drift, a starboard turn
Towards her sweating equator,
This shellback yearns.

A Pirate's Just Deserts

"Near this spot," it reads,
"They met their just deserts."
We twenty-nine hung,
We twenty-nine swung,
From an enigmatic oak
Content to hide now
Among its moss-draped kin.

Yet they thought enough of me
To carve my name in stone.
My year of just deserts as well,
And twenty-eight souls the same.
"A gentleman," it says.
But even so,
A pirate must be hung.

What mischief, malevolent deeds done
While led by a gentleman
Who must hang, of course,
Not from a sail draped mast,
Salt sprayed, wind whipped,
Free as fluttering tack;
But from a root anchored oak.

Was I not a patriot
Gallant, fearless,
Loved by crew,
Pleased many fair maidens, too?

Equally shared my dark-stained rum,
My blood the same sweet crimson?
So, must a gentleman be hung?

Hung we were.
While the crabs waited,
Patient as they were
For their portion due.
Low in the briny stew
Off the high Ba'tree
Where two rivers meet
To form the sea.

Waited there, deep they did,
Where sharp edged oysters clump
Round cast-off ballast stone.
Their graves, too, in the sulfuric muck.
Low water came, furled in its cover
To offer a soft pluff bed
For our twenty-nine dead.

Barbados born, I left all behind.
A gentleman pirate
Would suffice just fine
Until I dropped anchor
One last time and
Off Charleston Point
Lay down, one of twenty-nine.

Walk the Ba'tree now,
Look down on us
In the murky brine.
Our graves are there;
Somewhere lie we twenty-nine.
And say a prayer for ole Stede Bonnet,
My just deserts received in time.

A Heavenly 'Scape

It is indeed a heavenly 'scape,
But oh, so much more.
Its mistral wind sweeps clean the light
Where the Masters worked before.

The Alps rise far to the north,
Renoir white-snows their slopes.
The road turns through olive groves
Where Cezanne's touch gives hope.

White, feral horses lift their heads
To search for needed rains
Where van Gogh explored the pink salt lakes
In the dust of the Camargue Plains.

And does the Rhone kiss the canvas
With a color Matisse would wear?
St. Tropez waits on the Cote d'Azur,
Picasso adds his palette there.

Vineyards blend to lavender rows,
It's where Monet would play.
The river oils through heavy pines,
Marseille, a brush stroke away.

It is indeed a heavenly 'scape,
Your spire commands it so.
The Masters' spirits roam your frame,
Provence they can't let go.

Black Beauty

"Oh, I wish I was in the land of cotton:"

Betty, black Betty, black beauty.
Our 'waitee,' our 'waitress.'
She wore a thin, blue cotton dress
They all did, but hers, ahh,
Tighter at the curves, shorter,
Unbuttoned lower in the front.
She was our car washer
In our Cool Hand Luke movie,
And equally out of reach.
There was no hose to wet her thin dress
And reveal what lay shallow beneath,
No foamy white suds to press
Her breasts against, to tempt and tease.
But she did her job well.

"Old times there are not forgotten:"

Thousands to feed,
And all black women to do it.
Hungry white cadets, hungry for more than
What Betty brought to the table.
Big women, their Gullah clattered
Like crystal windchimes
Throughout the mess hall cathedral.
But there was work to do,
And the language changed

From bright colors to dull grey
When the Corps marched in, and then,
Time for Betty to wash the car.

"In Dixieland where I was born, early on a frosty morn:"

She was beyond my reach because
I did not reach. I lacked courage to reach.
Only my dreams had courage
To answer her seductive calls,
Touch her fine curves,
Embrace her sassy look,
Cut through the black and white decades.
And then the Confederate flag led our team
Onto the field and we sang "Dixie,"
Just once I wish I had touched her hand.

"Look away, look away, look away, Dixie land."

Finding Lynyrd Skynyrd

Where were you when
I needed "Whiskey Rock-A-Roller?"
Where was I
Through your fame and flame?
My incarcerated years helped
Hide your beards, long hair,
Your pounding rhythms
As I marched in line
Behind walls and bars.
I needed "Free Bird" then,
So, I could bang my head.

But I find you now,
Forty years late,
Burning new and bright.
Pugnacious Van Zant
Snarling out "Simple Man,"
Commanding the stage.
A cigarette clings
To King's lip, self-absorbed as he
Belts out the music
That escaped me then,
But sets my head banging now.

A plane took you down,
Ran out of fuel,
Landing gear down too soon,
And it caught the tall pines.

Why, why did you come down?
All down, all too soon.
Your music down, too,
Left high in the pines.
"They Call Me the Breeze"
Never made it to Baton Rouge
Where it would have set heads banging?

So many new songs
Spirited away in the wind.
And "Tuesday's Gone" for good.
And trees, like feverish fans,
So eager to reach up, touch them all,
And bring them down.
Unwritten songs left so high up
We will never find or hear them.
Treasures left high in the pines
That were too tall,
That would have our heads banging.

They Commanded the Mile

A small boy in my father's car,
I soaked up the back roads
Of our hot, summer lowlands.
He drove to a favorite place,
A stately road where many years before
One intrepid planter lined a sand road
With young sea island oaks,
Which through ages grew
Tall and full, grizzled with Spanish moss.
Strong limbs above embraced
As we tunneled through.
Massive trunks, inches away
From our smiles, And they…
They commanded the mile.

We paid tribute as we passed
With awed silence, witness to ancient oaks
Planted by one who knew the grandeur ahead,
Far beyond his years on earth.
Midday eclipsed into darker shade,
A tunnel of grey moss and green
Stretched out ahead
While the envious sun
Took a pitiful slice, here and there.
The mottled road engulfed
Our hood, dash, and hands.

We heard them whisper of other days
Of gentler ways when
Hooves danced on cool sand roads.
And years later, I could not find
This stately road to show my son.

Cut down. Cleared. Gone.

For a fool had decreed that they,
They who had commanded this mile,
Were too close to our smiles.

Ghost Car

We never saw a soul in the old, rust-red, ghost car
When it sputtered up the hill each afternoon,
Then disappeared down the far side.
We watched for it most days,
Squatted in the grass behind the wire fence.
Safe 'cept for nightmares we took home
To bed each night. Prayers didn't help.

It was an odd, old car even then.
"It's just an ole A Model"
Someone's father said.
But it did not need a name.
He should've just left it the ghost car.

We heard it long before we saw it,
A warning that steeled our resolve.
Forget and it'd catch you alone somewhere,
Send that extra shiver down your spine
That group courage helps ward off.

Once I dreamed a black man drove it.
Old, grey-stubbled with white hair,
Same color as the exhaust cloud
Out the back of the ghost car.
I figured it was all he could afford.
And once over the hill
He'd just coast down, quiet like,
Turn off on some dusty, dirt road,

Go somewhere we did not know,
Could not go.
I didn't know that place, even in my dream.

Maybe I dreamed it cause of Paul,
The black man who worked with my grandfather,
Whose truck had a thermos on the side,
One you had to put your mouth on,
Press a knob to get a cold drink.
They both used it the same.
I pressed the knob once just as
The ghost car coughed into view.
Paul said, "Look at that,
Ain't nobody driving that thing."
Then he winked at me.

Foothill Coyote

He howls and yaps and creeps.
Unseen in the misty hollows,
Along the silent creek,
Among the sturdy black walnuts
Edging out the fallow field.
Darkness cradles his voice,
Calling for who, for what?

I guess his lair and wish
To see flesh and fur
Of such a boastful beast,
Slinking, yet unafraid to take
A newborn calf, a careless
Yard dog, a foolish feline.

Endless bounty on you, my friend,
Fiend in the dark.
Howling, yelping, creeping,
Chilling my blood, conjuring
Thoughts of old movies
Black and white,
Like his night.

Do you dance in the dark,
Round a kill? Long for a mate?
Do you howl and yap and creep
Along secret paths, unseen
In the moonlit shadows, watching me
As I search for you?

I listen to your clear,
Ancient, visceral voice
Fill the hills and hollows.
Your night, your darkness, is mine.
The silvery shadows and
Secret paths are mine.
I will find you in the thick night.
It is where I, too, belong.

Bison on the Wall

The bison bore down
On the small "toe knocker" boy,
Who looked up in awe
At its massive head on the wall.
It was a bull from a different age
When their numbers thundered
And they roamed free
Across vast Nebraska plains.

The boy didn't need more
To know that what once stood
Behind this head was that of

A very large beast and
One look in its eyes felt fatal
As if facing head-on
A Greyhound bus with horns.

The bull's eyes stayed
With the boy as he grew
Through years of hard times.
They were eyes indifferent
To all but the boy
And drew him back
As a man where he found
The wall bare,
Empty as the plains.

But the man knew he would
Bring the bull back.
It remained on that wall
Clear in his mind, through it all.

Then the bull found its way
Down his spine, out his living fingers
And onto the starved canvas;
Alive again to lead
Those dark flowing rivers of bison
That once churned from
Montana to Texas.

He gripped the bull's
Head and horns
Like a rodeo bulldogger,
Wrestled him to the ground,
Tied his legs together,
Then raised his own hand.
His wife declared him winner,
Hung the bull on the wall
And will not let it go again.

Death of a War Correspondent

I find her in the photo lying prone along a trail
Where she has bled and died.
I know this, not by the caption,
But by the sheen of what has pooled around her neck.
It is the last photo on the last page of his collection,
A posthumous book tribute to her life's work as a
War Correspondent.
It is the only photo in his collection
She did not take.

A trip wire and mine found her
Where the slosh of Vietnam
Rice paddies and sharp-edged elephant grass merge.
Her bush hat lies close by, blown clear by the blast.
It was her calling card,
Like her horn-rimmed glasses and
Pearl earrings from Tehran.
They all went home with her.
The photo, like all of hers, is black and white,

Best to tell the stark contrast between life and death,
The fine line she bravely walked for a very long time.
Beside her kneels a Navy Chaplain,
There to deliver last rights.
Marines stand behind,
Saddened by yet another death.
She was one of their own and
War took its sweet time to kill her.

His book title reads *Dickey Chapelle Under Fire,*
First American Female War Correspondent
Killed in Action. It is not a book or title she sought.
But she knew well the risks,
Had always burned glass ceilings,
Pushed and clawed into the brutal,
Closely guarded realms of men,
Unafraid as sniper rounds buzzed past her
Like irritant wasps
In the desolate bomb craters of
Iwo Jima and Okinawa.

"No place for a woman," the generals had said.
She once befriended Michener on the bridge at Andau
Where they both told the world how the Hungarians
Fled Soviet occupation and brutality.
Arrested by communists, she stood steadfast,
Endured the anguish of interrogation, uncertainty,

And seclusion in the infamous Fo Street Prison.
She feared not the French and secreted her way
Into the Algerian rebel camps to speak for them.
She, a woman among Arabs. She, their voice,
Their message silenced prior as if the Sahara
Had conspired to mute their cause.

She eluded Batista's secret police,
Worked her way into
Cuba's rugged Sierra Maestra,
Where she sat beside Castro
And reported on yet another exploding revolution.

Exposed to the harsh realities of life in caves and
combat and the relentless discomfort
Offered free by an indifferent jungle,
She wrote, photographed,
And reported the raw truth as she saw it.

Soldiers and Marines mourned her death.
She was one of their own, a love and honor
Bestowed on few save their brothers,
Those damn few who fought and died beside them.
Her biography title reads *Fire in the Wind*, and
She truly was "Fire in the Wind" to the very end.

Wyoming Hunt

Blue smoke rose from the far horizon
Climbed smooth and high,
Covered him like a soft blanket
Pulled up and over, but in false comfort.
He turned often into the wind
Like a pointer, stiff on quail,
To search for the acrid scent
Of a grass fire thought drifting his way.

But news came
That a hay barn burned
On a far ranch which would be
Trouble for their cattle come
Winter when a white blanket
Softened the land.

And far off, an antelope
Stood tall below the ridge.

Through the glass his large eyes flashed,
Stared back with theater eyes,
A seasoned actor, his stage,
A vast endless brown of
Muscular hills with strong shoulders,
Hiding their oasis of clear, cold streams,
Gnarled cottonwoods, tough as the
Rock clutched by their roots.

He shared his one act play
With an audience of one.
Windmills, far off and alone,
Claimed stage left and right as
Lone cattle wandered, indifferent
To the dance of the first scene.
He hid his herd below the hill,
His backstage. Then,
He pushed them out.

They raced like thoroughbreds on home stretch,
Flew like a ship's flag in a gale,
Its colors, black, white, and tan.
Masculine colors of the land.
Resolute in his flight and
Undeterred by the high, thin air.
He knew well, life is not fair.

So, the hunter pursued,
And the play endured.
One horn had an odd angle,
Like a wayward prop seen only
By the audience. He was unaware.
It made him special, rare,
Worth the stalk in rarefied air,
To crawl, to scratch up the hill and
Across the dry plain to peer

Over and through the scope as
Crosshairs brought him close.
The audience of one braced hard.
Angle and range, good.
Breath stopped. Found his heart.
Made the shot.
Then actor and curtain fell while
The audience of one
Picked up his empty shell.

An Oasis

The small town is cold-vacant.
Its people driven away
By war and the promise
Of a long-range missile
Carrying hideous gifts.

We intrude the quiet,
Not even a barking dog.
An occasional leaf, breeze blown,
Scrapes down the street.
It should all be bleak, black, and white,
Like an old silent movie, or a walk on a London Street
Late night in fog. But it is not.

Rules are gone.
Even the scent of life has left.
No diesel exhaust taints the air
From overloaded lorries.
No baking bread wafting
Down narrow, shadowed lanes,
Crying to be stabbed in hummus.
No oiled ladies upwind,
To tempt and torture our starved souls.
It is good that none of this is here.

A lime green building appears
In the late evening, sun low,
Shadows dance on its face

From tall, long-limbed trees.
It might be French design. I want it to be.
I am glad its humble; two stories
Offer a peaceful facade, unscathed.
There are no scars. It has escaped
The trauma of war.

We enter a grand front entrance
To an old orphanage for girls,
A name we change to women,
Smirk, and imagine.
It's been a while.
We imagine their laughter, smiles,
Their shy, inquisitive ways.
We see their governesses usher them away.

We go in, cautious, but unafraid,
For we hold death in our hands.
He leads, I follow; he knows the way,
He was here before, found it,
Now shares it, but only with me.

The piano sits center, alone,
In the spacious room.
Silent, majestic, in need.
There his soul rests and drinks.
I hear his music
Long before he plays.
I see young girls gathered
Around as if to pray,
To gush at his handsome face,

Blush when he turns his blond head
And their eyes meet, and they dream.

His weapon hits heavy, metallic, on the floor,
Indifferent to all of this
And rudely intrudes, like us.
We accept the risk. And he sits and plays.
The keys light the dim room,
Echoes out the open door
Which I watch closely,
But I want to close my eyes.
The notes spill out like water from an oasis
Filling the empty city for a moment,
Giving life to the trees and flowers
And the orphaned girls who
Run in to gather at water's edge and drink.
And we are all sweetly deceived.

El Paisano

He ripped the longhorns off the pink Cadillac
Parked outside the El Paisano Hotel,
Stormed past the courtyard, to the bar
To throw back more angry shots of Tequila.

Once outside, thick darkness cloaked him in dread
As an endless net of stars draped his world.
The soothing sounds of the fountain faded
As he swayed a long walk home.

A distant dull glow was his siren song
Which led to a dark place where the wind cut hard.
He sat, wedged in, as his world spun on;
Woke to the cold, put on his friend's oversized shoes,

Stumbled out with clown feet, into the growing light
Where tall saguaro stared down without pity.
They had seen it too many times before.
But a cold horchata revived his hunter spirit.

And the shy, Barbary sheep climbed high that day
And the rocks begrudged his every step.
And the rattlers lay dormant in the cold;
And the only poison lay far below.

He looked down on the El Paisano
As it napped in the dusty flats below.
But he could not find the hornless Cadillac
In the crosshairs of his scope.

Sweet Horchata

You saved me, sweet Horchata,
When morning light came too quick, too bright
And our tequila-fueled stars left without farewell,
No more to flash and writhe like
A seine net fat with silver minnows
Framed under a full moon's light.

You fueled my morning hunt, sweet Horchata,
When hungry hogs plowed earth
Round the corn pile while white-thick fog
Hid all but their eager grunts.
And high in rough, cinnamon rocks I dreamed
A lion waited, like me, for the clearing lift.

You slowed my heart, sweet Horchata,
When my glass found the Barbary Sheep,
But far too high, too early, where
They clung to rock face like Velcro.
My glass brought them close but
Deceived the hard work that lay ahead.

You stiffened my resolve, sweet Horchata,
To climb high where they led us. But
They are nimble and pragmatic,
Applied their ancient African instincts
To elude us and left us
Wanting on the steep slopes.

You quenched my thirst, sweet Horchata,
Joined me in sweat-stained shade
To lean against the mountain's back,
Share its precious view which
No camera can capture,
No memory can fully recall.

Then you abandoned me, sweet Horchata.
The long descent steep, guns, and packs heavy,
Our steps carefully applied. Stars came back, too.
But they were not tequila-fueled.
And a heavy weight came again
To lay on my shoulders where
I hung it long before I found you,
Sweet Horchata.

Something of Value

Imperiled pachyderm, modern mastodon,
You are a storm through thick bush:
Make roads through high grass,
Tunnels through thorned acacias;
You and yours are a grey river at dusk
Flowing on the far horizon.

You gently nudge
The bleached bones of your dead.
You know them.
You do not forget them.
Your tears have far to drop

To water the deepest dust of Africa.
We feel your inner rumblings
Of grief and despair.
They are ours, too.

But later you will be found,
A wire cut deep in a leg
Like a sable palm,
Holes in your sun-dried hide,
Where death entered,
Life flowed out and blackness
And lifeless plains followed.

Your white ivory gone,
Replaced by stark black holes
Which stare back.
While somewhere,
Soulless artists carve,
And we safely marvel at the scene
Carved in your tusks that once fought
Fierce lions, towering bulls
But could not shield small bullets.

And what remains?
You are absorbed in the fallow ground
And orange dust
Where only your bleached bones
Hold something of value.

What I Learned from Chip

He pushed his helmet back
Off his forehead,
Unhooked his chin strap.
It dangled haphazard, loose
Down the sides of his face.
He wore a weary,
Seasoned look and never smiled.
How could he with all those
Tombstones in his eyes?

Combat starring Vic Morrow
As Sergeant "Chip" Saunders.
Just call him Vic?
I liked Vic, a strong name,
A man's name.
'Chip' reminded me
Of the slow, fat kid
On *My Three Sons*.

But Chip was tough.
Each week he did his duty
In a black & white box filled
With all the greyness of life.
A scowl, a crooked mouth
Spoke clearly through fear.
His sardonic voice spoke
Truth for the silent.

Then all week
I fought to play Chip,
Fought to be Chip,
Carry the Tommy Gun,
Replay the battles
In our woods and fields.
I was seven.
Thought I knew his world.

But I had not yet
Solved the dilemmas,
Forgiven human vulnerability.
I was not yet weary.
Then suddenly, he was gone,
As if I had changed channels.
A *Twilight Zone* movie
Took him away.

It is hard to find Vic now.
He is as elusive
As those woods and fields
I once roamed so freely.
The black-and-white has faded, too,
Overcome by greyness which engulfs and grows,
Disguised as vivid colors.
And no one fights anymore
To carry the Tommy Gun like Chip?

Late Confession

It has long bothered me
That we shot them in their bed.
A cold, rainy day, when the clouds
Hung low and pinched us in.

We left with guns in hand, a thirst to kill,
A mission to fulfil,
Slogged through thick wood,
Cursed the briar that bloodied our thighs
And tried in vain to slow our stride.

The hours passed and the empty miles,
Then their small home rose high above.
We could see well enough, unbothered
By limbs that swayed in the frosted breeze.

We tried to flush them out
With shouts and un-aimed shots
But it was best they stayed inside
Where it was warm and dry
And a better place to die.

It seems now so long ago that
No one really gave an order and
No single one can you blame.
For we all shot; we all aimed.

And their house fell, far,
Hit with a thud.
We peeled away the dry,
The warmth, the soft inside.
Two squirrels embraced
And that thought has always stayed.

Eva Braun's Home Movies

You are a lithe-limbed muliebral,
A sunflower lighting the darkness
Of your own home movies.
You are the only one in color,
All others blurred black and white;
Their images burn, crumble, and die.
Are you just a foolish child,
Innocent, deceived, too, by their lies,
Blind to the horror around you?
Or committed to love evil?

You would have been my world.
We would not have seen war,
Wanted other nations, a continent.
Just flowers, robust and vibrant colors,
Like you, in your film,
All black and white images gone,
Turned to ash, in place of the millions.

Show me again your slim youth,
Your sweet smile.
Pout like a child, for me.
Pick more flowers, just for me.
Swim longer in the cold sea and
Pose again on the wall, for me.
Lie warm beside the lake again.
Stop the film, step out of the frame,
Take my hand. Walk away with me.

And the world will never wonder
What drew you to the world
He set on fire. And you,
Forever a footnote to his evil.

My Shot 'a Whiskey

I would rather write than read.
But when I read, I can write.
Like a shot 'a whiskey
Makes it right,
Helps me write it right,
And somehow clears the light
And the words become light
As a crow's feather
Found on a cold, dark night.
That is when you know
You have it right.
You go home, sit tight,
And write it right.
"Write it right" I say.
Read some, then you can write.
And that shot 'a whiskey
Will make it right.
Will make it all right.

Honeymoon Pull-Off

It was a place in the sun to pull off,
Shed the remnants of their day:
Sweep out the irritant rice grains,
Cut loose the noisy cans, twisted string,
Wipe clean the words greased on glass,
All to celebrate their first
Of thousands more together.

Now, she points out the spot,
Clearly remembered
From that youthful road
That led into unknown curves
With miles of days and years ahead.
And today, they dare look back
And see it all so clearly flash by.

I park and walk this same spot,
Search in secret for those old cast offs,
Knowing they are not there.
But hoping I find them new again.
I find no words.
And I cannot write them again
On my window.

I want them to pull off again,
Start that day again,
Hold that day forever again,
Share that life together again

And drive again, into that long unknown
And not look back,
Move again around the curves ahead
And speak again those words,
Washed away so long ago
Where they pulled off
And where I now stand
And where behind me now,
They hold each other's weathered hands
While my tears drop and wet the sand.

Winter Beach

I trundle along among your indigent,
Sand in my shoes,
Pepper trees plague your landscape
Sculpted by sun-bleached flowers.
Colors pop from kind angels
Whose homes mingle
With contented spirits left to wander
When their sanctuary walked away,
Left them like an unwanted pet
Put out on the roadside, an easy riddance.

It is Winter Beach.
Things wash ashore here
And linger for want of someone
To take them away,
Unlike those mossy stones of Scotland,
Serious and dour,
Or the crypts of Paris,
Or those chaotic layers of history
Found in the Jews' graves of Prague
And rigid rows of Arlington.

You are homespun, simple,
Fitting for your guests and those
Who found a sedate corner to rest.
Ancient graves.... no, but as wholly
American as cowboy boots.
There is no order here; poorly marked,
You eschew labels, expectations while
Your stoic statues welcome silly dolls and
Where the well-traveled are as welcome
As your indigent.

The Banshee

She sat straight up in bed,
Screamed like a Banshee, "He's dead!"
These words unnerved all who ran to her,
Unnerved all those close to her the rest of her life.
Late in that black night
Her voice echoed thru the decaying,
High-ceilinged house
Which now felt haunted, became haunted.
Whatever she dreamed, whatever she then knew,
Soon proved painfully true.

She knew. She saw it clearly: his fatal wreck.
Orange flames vivid and hot
Shot from the bloody noses of two cars, embraced
Head on, like two boxers clinched in a corner.
She saw the sharp, splintered glass on her heavy quilt,
Scattered there from shattered windshields.
She felt the angry road gravel scrape her knees.
The red wetness weakened her as
She bled out on the hot asphalt.

It was hers but not hers,
His.
He was far away, headed home,
Gone too long for what work could be found.
Too eager to see his daughter.
Eager to speed.
And the Banshee screamed.

Petrol in a Puddle

The storm came, lashed, and left
Its mark on many, mostly me.
Puddles dotted the street.
Dark asphalt, soaked blacker,
Exhaled a vaporous mist
Like a left hook to a boxer's jaw.
Petrol, dripped from a passing car,
Spread out in the puddle,
Colors running like a rainbow in water.
He stood brooding on the steps,
Large, dark, a length
Of something in his hand.
One end made a handle
To grip, swing and bruise.
A bottle, tossed aside in the grass.
Its cap lost but a little something remained
Clear and brown in the bottom.
An intoxicating aroma,
Even for a boy.

I will taste it one day.
But not today, for I have puddles to splash
And my welts will swell and gain colors
Like the petrol in the puddle.

What's Uncle Worth

The last time I saw him
He sat on his horse, tall in the saddle.
A sweat-stain ringed his weathered hat.
He looked like a Confederate cavalryman,
Just needed a colorful peacock feather
To add some flair.

He spoke the speed of black-strap molasses,
Walked even slower, like a bow-legged Robert Duval
Lonesome Dove double. But the real thing.
Did not trust banks since the Great Depression.
So, he buried his money in mason jars
All over his farm.
Most of 'em still out there.

At times he was a mean and indifferent sonovabitch.
But he was always glad to see me.
Did not care a lick for what others thought.
That's what I liked most about him:
His honest indifference to the world.
He was his own man of simple but strong passions:

Cattle, horses, hot biscuits, and moonshine.
He dairy-farmed most of his life,
A job with no break. Cows gotta be milked every day.
Said he retired when at eighty-five
He shifted from dairy to beef cattle.
Like shifting from Formula One to NASCAR.

Then Black Angus dotted his green pastures,
A nice contrast of two rich colors on a giant canvas.
Barn odors intoxicated like landscape paint fumes:
Elixir of hay, sweet feed, stale milk, and cow shit;
True smells of the earth
You could taste in the air.
White milk flowed through overhead glass tubes,

The blood through his veins. Its heart,
A large stainless vat, alive as it hummed
And churned and chilled. Cold and full of fat,
The milk tasted like a drink from the gods
In the summer heat that stifled us in that barn.
Each spring he brought in a stud bull.
Kept him in a pen so tight he couldn't turn around,
But close enough to know why he was there.
And we could not resist the chance
To torment a penned-up bull.
We tortured his giant scrotum,
Made his eyes bulge with rage
As he slung snot and horned his pen,
Trying to get one in us.
He'd kill us given half a chance.

I surprised Uncle Worth one Sunday as
He sat on his porch and twirled a loaded pistol.
He didn't attend church often
But he'd gone that morning.
He'd sat on the inside back pew and waited,
Waited for the preacher to finish and
Come down the aisle.

Then he stood up and socked the preacher in the jaw.

The preacher had wronged him somehow.
We never knew how.
I do not think I have ever heard of
A preacher punched in church.
But Uncle Worth did, and
He did not give a second thought
How this might jeopardize his eternal soul.
As long as he had cattle, horses,
Biscuits, and moonshine,
He was as close to heaven as he ever needed to be.

Apple Tree Dreams

In the tall, thick apple tree
We played out the past,
Forged our dreams for free
And like the fall winds
Our futures came fast
And dreams fell like exhausted fruit.

Yet some clung, high above,
Hesitant to end it all
With a simple fall
Where their fragrant death
Would strengthen the ground
And feed the bees
Who sucked their final life's gift.

Far below, the dead
And dying lay all around.
We saw both, above and below.
Those clinging, to be eaten, savored
And those below.
We breathed their last sweet
Fragrance of life and
Remembered them, all.

Grandma Squaw

My Grandma was an Indian Squaw.
Well, that is what I was always told.
She looked it: high cheekbones,
Brown-leathery face, white hair.
Yea, you're offended by those words "Indian Squaw."
Fuck you. I like 'em. More noble, warrior-like.
She gave me Indian blood.
So, I'll damn well use them if I want.

Grandma Squaw never talked much.
When she did, I listened.
I heard my ancestors in her voice.
In an old photo, she sits on their back porch steps
With her father, my great-grandfather, Ben Miller.
My Dad knew Ben.
Said Ben didn't take shit off nobody.

He looked it, too: proud, dark,
A chiseled face with a hat on.
Cherokee, Catawba, not sure, but I'll find it one day.
Wish I had known him but he died too young.
His four daughters didn't take shit
Off nobody neither.
Once Grandma Squaw broke a switch off a tree limb,
Used it to get my attention. It worked.

You can make a damn good switch with a small,
Maple tree branch. Stings like hell on bare legs.

Then she fed me her sweet potato pie.
Best I ever had. But that recipe is gone.
Near the end, she sat on the couch and read a lot.
Read a lot of books. Smiled and laughed a lot, too.

Once, I opened a door to a dark,
Empty room in her house.
Thought I saw a man lying on the floor.
Big duffle bags lay on the floor, and in the dark
Looked like a strange, dead man.
Scared hell outta me.
She saw me jump and scream like a scalded cat.
She talked about that until she died.
Never stopped laughing 'bout it.

I didn't get home to say goodbye before she died.
But the man at the funeral home let me see her.
She lay on her back on the embalming table,
Like on a funeral pyre.
I touched her cold, high cheeks,
Brown leathery face, and white hair.
Her Indian spirit rose off that table, hugged me,
Said goodbye.
Later, I sat on the back porch steps with my dad,
Her son.

Admired his proud, dark, chiseled face.
People often said he looked like Charles Bronson.
He didn't take shit off nobody neither.
When they said that,
My Dad just pointed his finger and
Pulled the trigger.

Strength of Odysseus

Your fangs are not those of a viper,
Your venom, not fatal but quick.
Your bright colors gave fair warning.
Your bite simply made his soul sick.

You slithered out of the darkness.
Your youth made your bands bright and bold.
Your eyes burned thru his innocent soul.
Your red touched your yellow band of gold.

You are, indeed, a snake with venom. But
You must chew on your victim awhile.
You are captured here in artistic form.
Your poison, just part of your guile.

He did not heed all your warnings.
He did not hear his own clear voice.
He did not keep a fair distance.
He simply made the wrong choice.

You are the serpent in the Garden of Eden.
You are the Siren he could not resist. And
When illness and drink dulled his senses,
He lost his Odysseus strength.

The Fall

He fell.
The big Bay fell.
"No, not the strong one!"
"He'd never fall!" they yelled.
But the jockey was new.
Her colorful silks and youth prevailed
Against better judgement and loyal strength.
And the Bay was ill.
And on a long downhill,
She led him too fast.
Her grip on his reigns too tight.
His head too high, his sight impaired,
And though he cleared the hedge with ease,
Stumbled from its backside water, and fell.
He stumbled.
He fell.

So many courses run,
So many races won,
So many hills climbed and hedges cleared,
But now a blemish, this sin, this fall.
He'd cleared so many, till now.
But now, not all.

The Forgiving River

He said forgiveness is a path,
A road to travel,
Not a line to cross,
Not a door to close behind;
For the door can be heavy,
The line a crevasse, a canyon, a gulf;
And there are many to forgive,
There is much to forget.
But are there too many roads,
Too many paths
Laced with regret?

We are told to forgive, but not how.
It is not a cleansing
Like a dive in a clear, cool lake
Or a laid-back baptism,
A nose-held dunk in preachers' hands.
Not mist rising from a warm pond
On a cold morning,
Or the whisper of wind
Through yesterday's pines.

Or is it
A frantic swim against the river's current
Sweeping toward high falls
Downstream, swift,
Then over in the tumult, the spray,
The cold plunge into swirling depths,

Like the rush of going over
Niagara in a barrel?

Perhaps I can press on, not forgive?
Carry it, float awhile,
A long while, in the gentle sweep
Of a lazy river, going somewhere,
With me along.
It's as good as any road, any path.
And I shall take it,
And tuck my forgiveness
Under my arm for a while.

Sail On

She feared the wild places
In my heart.
She cared not for my adventures,
Or sought comfort in exotic realms
Where I dreamed.

She dared not explore
Beyond the near border
But saw clearly that I would.
Her beauty beckoned, held me.
I could not shed it then.

But it grew ever distant
As my ship sailed on.
And I found
On a far western shore,
A love to last.

One to weather my misadventures,
Share my far-off realms.
We explored the world
Together, with billowed sails.
And a light ahead, on a distant shore
Grows ever brighter
As our ship sails on.

My Suzanne

She was my Aphrodite;
I longed to be her Mars.
She rose from the surf's foam,
Took hold my weathered hand.
I have not let go.
Other shores left unexplored;
Hers, the only one I need know.

Eyes I'd not seen before
Spoke our future long ago,
When ambrosia fueled our lust
And was our daily feast.
Her arrow pierced my heart,
A tender kiss, my soul.
I was gladly laid low.

Then my ship sailed into gales;
She stood patient on the shore.
Her firm hand always there;
I felt it on the wheel.
My course plotted home,
Of that I made sure,
For only her star guided me.

Once home, I laid down
My sword and my shield.
And beside her again
Her soft brown eyes said all,
Until harm's way again did call;
"Go slay miscreant dragons
Or not come back at all."

But my sword proved worthy and
I carried my own shield home.
But hers were forged with stronger steel
And I no longer fought alone.
Then when life's arrows swiftly flew,
Beside me, Aphrodite walked and
We fought them all, we two.

Dropping Anchor

Aye mate,

Ye stand in the threshold of a Sailor's new home.
He's traded his sea legs for a banker's loan.
Inside you'll find his wife, a Saint,
And two fine children, tough as armor plate.
His beer's as cold as a missionary wife,
With a deep draft head, froth of a Sailor's fight.
His rum is as stiff as a monsoon in May,
His language as salty as South China Sea spray.

Now if there be more than one mate inside,
Ye must weather their tales
Until well past full tide.
And if ye be weak and easily offended
By the colorful language of the mates he's befriended,
Then be bold, step inside, and hoist one for fun.
Or move on to starboard, mate,
And not waste their rum!

About the Author

Michael is a former Naval Officer and Navy SEAL who served over twenty-six years on active duty, a career which afforded him an opportunity to work in fifteen different countries. His focused areas of the Western Pacific and Persian Gulf region presented great adventures in exotic Asian and Arabic cultures. He was awarded a Bronze Star during Desert Storm among numerous other personal awards during a long and illustrious career. He shares time at his home in Florida, his North Carolina farm, and Scotland. He continues to pursue his passions to write, hunt, and travel.

Notes

"Where the Moss Don't Grow"
In my first book, *The Lightning and the Gale,* I changed the poem by using more vernacular dialect than was in the original poem. I like the original much better. Not sure why I changed it. So, this is the original.

"Nora, A Student's Lament"
A tribute to a favorite teacher. She was exotic, erotic, sophisticated, and a lovely European intellectual. She's one of the few I vividly remember.

"I Dream Again of You"
A poetic version of a dream about a first love. What sparks a dream like this after so many years?

"Night Blooming Jasmine"
My young son planted Jasmine at the base of a tall pine in our yard. It grew to engulf the entire tree. When in bloom, its fragrance filled the street and intoxicated all who walked by. This poem embellishes an incident when a neighbor happened by one evening and stopped to inhale the jasmine's unique perfume.

"Ode to Cleavage"
What red-blooded hetero male doesn't like the sight of that wonderful, awe-inspiring crevasse, one of God's greatest gifts? Too bad we can't stare and must resort

to stealing glances. I suppose we could stare, but it's considered rude as well as rather risky!

"Flower of Calvary"
An ekphrastic poem inspired by a stained-glass image by artist Anita Prentis. It conveys the simple facts, data, and story lore of my favorite tree, the Royal Poinciana.

"She Carried the Scent of Coffee"
I met an old friend for coffee once. She was fighting cancer and had just finished a round of chemo. She texted me later that the aroma of that coffee and coffee shop stayed with her through the day. I wish that scent had the power to cure.

"Rose Dew"
This poem recalls an evening spent with a lovely girl at a quaint cottage beside the salt marsh on the Vernon River in Georgia. I wondered at the time if we would spend a lifetime together. (The girl, not the cottage.)

"The Crystal Wind Chime"
Time stood still at this remote ferry landing somewhere in the Outer Banks of North Carolina. It was warm, quiet, empty of people, and the wind chime was the only sound. It was one of those rare days, sounds, and moments that are permanently tattooed in my memory.

"My Virgin Chart"
I love the old paper charts and the mysteries, secrets, and promises of adventure they hold. The poem also takes on somewhat of an erotic tone. And why not?

"A Pirate's Just Deserts"
A tribute to the iconic pirate, Stede Bonnet, and his crew, all hanged along the lovely Battery (aka "Ba'tree") in Charleston, South Carolina. Pirates, how can you not love 'em? And yes, the spelling of "Deserts" is correct.

"A Heavenly Scape"
My ekphrastic poem inspired by a painting by artist Laura Reed Howell. It's of a scene in Provence, France, an area renowned for its beauty and unique light, an area much preferred by many famous and gifted artists.

"Black Beauty"
At The Citadel, the entire corps eats all meals at the same time. When I was there during the 1970s, all the waitresses, aka "waitees" who prepared the tables, served the food, and cleared the tables, were black. Most of them spoke Gullah, and their vibrant, colorful conversations before the cadets marched in were magical, although mostly unintelligible to us. Betty was one of these waitresses. She was younger than the others, very lovely, and sassy. Her uniform blue cotton dress showed her curves. She knew she was the object

of our desire but off limits for many reasons, primarily our many fears.

"Finding Lynyrd Skynyrd"
I rediscovered this remarkable band. What a tragedy to lose them and the promise they held.

"They Commanded the Mile"
These were remarkable old trees. The idiot that had them cut down should be hung, drawn, and quartered. An inexcusable act that still makes me angry.

"Ghost Car"
I can still see and hear the old car sputtering up the hill and feel the hair on the back of my neck stand up just thinking about it. Such a simple childhood thrill that had the power to unite a group of kids.

"Foothill Coyote"
The night howls of the coyotes around our farm are haunting and beautiful. They are crafty, resilient canines, and they are hunted unmercifully. I love them for their elusive success and their mysterious MO. Their nightly group yelp sessions are just their way of giving us the finger. The most glorious howls are from loners.

"Bison on the Wall"
My ekphrastic poem inspired by a painting of a Bison's head and its unique backstory as told by its artist, Eldon Lux.

"Death of a War Correspondent"
This is about the death of Dickey Chapelle, a female war correspondent killed in Vietnam. It is rare for Soldiers and Marines in the field to revere a person of the media, much less a female media rep. But she was welcomed and loved by these warriors from WWII through numerous global conflicts until her untimely death while on a patrol with Soldiers in Vietnam. I never met her, but she is my hero. Her life is a fascinating story of a woman overcoming so many obstacles to succeed in a man's world. Hers is the story of a woman who defied convention and did things her way. My own mother was like this, too.

"Wyoming Hunt"
Wyoming is beautiful, rugged, and big. The entire state is less populated than the city of San Diego. It is a harsh and unforgiving place populated with big animals, tough people, and unforgettable landscapes. I even have a large mounted sailfish on my wall that came from Wyoming. That story is best explained with a shot 'a whiskey! It is a unique place indeed.

"An Oasis"
During a patrol through a (hopefully) deserted Arab town, my buddy suddenly and unexpectedly diverted us for a moment to a lovely building. Somehow, he knew there was a piano inside. We went in, and he played for a while. It was beautiful, soothing, haunting, and totally out of place for the situation. I'll

never forget it, nor the look of pleased satisfaction on his face as if he'd just given the war a middle finger.

"El Paisano"
A poem inspired by a dinner at the iconic El Paisano Hotel in the small West Texas town of Marfa. It's an eclectic town where the cast of the movie *Giant* stayed during filming. The cast included James Dean, Rock Hudson, Elizabeth Taylor, and many other famous actors, including one of my favorites, a young Dennis Hopper.

"Sweet Horchata"
I first had this lovely drink in a small southwest Texas town while hunting Barbary Sheep at a nearby ranch. It was (is) the perfect anecdote for a rough Tequila hangover.

"Something of Value"
My first ekphrastic poem inspired by a photo from accomplished photographer Jennifer Johnson. It is simply an emphasis on the beauty and sad fate of the majestic African elephant.

"What I Learned from Chip"
This poem is a tribute to the old TV series *Combat* and its main star, Vic Morrow. It seems we've lost more than Vic in recent years.

"Late Confession"
Funny how a boyhood hunt stays with you and how insignificant, or conversely significant, two dead squirrels might seem.

"Eva Braun's Home Movies"
I watch those series about the Nazis and will occasionally see the silly home movies made by, and of, Eva Braun. I cannot fathom how such a young, lovely woman accepted and endured all the evil around her. Was she equally evil? I cannot get my head around so much evil and so much indifference to it.

"My Shot 'a Whiskey"
A silly, whimsical poem. But a shot 'a whiskey does smooth out many edges.

"Honeymoon Pull Off"
The last Mother's Day I spent with my mother, I found myself on the same drive they had taken just after their wedding in 1950. They pulled off the road to shed the things tied to their car before continuing on with their honeymoon. I pulled off at that exact spot and was overcome with emotion at being with them 70 years later, at that exact same spot which my mother had not forgotten. Of all the poems in this collection, I can't read this one without choking up.

"Winter Beach"
This ekphrastic poem was inspired by a report of a visit to the Winter Beach Cemetery by Louise Kennedy when she was the Executive Director of the Laura (Riding) Jackson Foundation. I was struck by the beauty of her description and transformed it into a poem for her initially. The cemetery is where Laura and her husband, Schuyler B. Jackson, are buried. It is indeed an iconic cemetery.

"The Banshee"
My mother's father, my grandfather, was killed in a car wreck when she was six. She woke in the night at the time of his wreck and knew it had happened. She had this sixth sense about her that could unnerve all at times. But it was a special gift.

"Petrol in a Puddle"
A fabricated event, although the rainbow sheen produced by petroleum in water is always fascinating. But it's a nightmare for a Naval Officer when seen near a ship.

"What's Uncle Worth"
My Uncle Worth (my maternal grandmother's brother) was a crazy, hard-working, and tough man. He got crazier, harder-working, and tougher the older he got. But he was unique, and I still miss him.

"Apple Tree Dreams"
We lived in Asheville, North Carolina, when I was young. It was a magical place with woods and fields right up against our house. This was paradise for a young boy. Several old apple trees provided a favorite hang-out where we could climb high and dream big.

"Grandma Squaw"
There are strong Native American genes in our ancestral lineage on my paternal grandmother's side. A photo of her father, Ben, my great-grandfather, shows a man who has the features of Jim Thorpe.

"Strength of Odysseus"
An ekphrastic poem inspired by a sculpture of a Coral Snake by Sean Sexton, Poet Laureate of Indian River County, Florida.

"The Fall"
A metaphor best left to your imagination.

"The Forgiving River"
There are some in our lives we find difficult to forgive. The challenge is to reconcile forgiving others with accepting forgiveness. If we can't or won't forgive, how can we be forgiven? This is, by definition, a dilemma.

"Sail On"
"My Suzanne"
"Dropping Anchor"
These three poems are more personal. My wife - the solid ship beneath my tattered sails.

Thank you for Reading *The Impeded Stream*
Please post a review for the author on Amazon.com

Other Books by Michael R. Howard

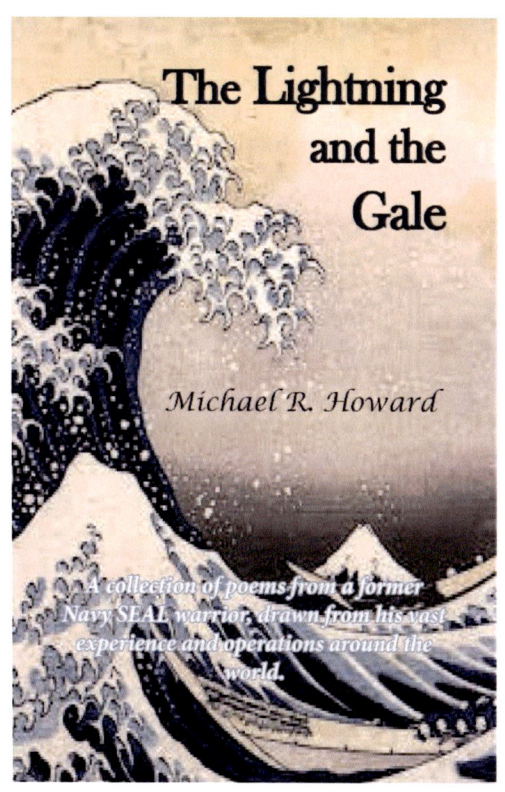

www.ingramcontent.com/pod-product-compliance
Lightning Source LLC
Chambersburg PA
CBRC102100150426
43199CB00007B/32